MEATS

The majority of the cuts of meat which are kosher are those which require long, slow cooking. These cuts of meat are the most nutritious ones and by long, slow cooking can be made as acceptable as the more expensive cuts of meat; they are best boiled or braised.

In order to shut in the juices the meat should at first be subjected to a high degree of heat for a short time. A crust or case will then be formed on the outside, after which the heat should be lowered and the cooking proceed slowly.

This rule holds good for baking, where the oven must be very hot for the first few minutes only; for boiling, where the water must be boiling and covered for a time, and then placed where it will simmer only; for broiling, where the meat must be placed close to the red-hot coals or under the broiler flame of the gas stove at first, then held farther away.

Do not pierce the meat with a fork while cooking, as it makes an outlet for the juices. If necessary, to turn it, use two spoons.

PAN ROAST BEEF

Take a piece of cross-rib or shoulder, about two and one-half to three pounds, put in a small frying-pan with very little fat; have the pan very hot, let the meat brown on all sides, turning it continually until all sides are done, which will require thirty minutes altogether. Lift the meat out of pan to a hot platter, brown some onions, serve these with the meat.

AN EASY POT ROAST

Take four pounds of brisket, season with salt, pepper and ginger, add three tablespoons of tomatoes and an onion cut up. Cover with water in an iron pot and a close-fitting cover, put in oven and bake from three to four hours.

POT ROAST. BRAISED BEEF

Heat some fat or goose fat in a deep iron pot, cut half an onion very fine and when it is slightly browned put in the meat. Cover up closely and let the meat brown on all sides. Salt to taste, add a scant half teaspoon of paprika, half a cup of hot water and simmer an hour longer, keeping covered closely all the time. Add one-half a sweet green pepper (seeds removed), one small carrot cut in slices, two tablespoons of tomatoes and two onions sliced.

Two and a half pounds of brisket shoulder or any other meat suitable for pot roasting will require three hours slow cooking. Shoulder of lamb may also be cooked in this style.

When the meat is tender, remove to a warm platter, strain the gravy, rubbing the thick part through the sieve and after removing any fat serve in a sauce boat.

If any meat is left over it can be sliced and warmed over in the gravy, but the gravy must be warmed first and the meat cook for a short time only as it is already done enough and too much cooking will render it tasteless.

BRISKET OF BEEF (BRUSTDECKEL)

If the brisket has been used for soup, take it out of the soup when it is tender and prepare it with a horseradish sauce, garlic sauce or onion sauce. (See "Sauces for Meats".)

BRISKET OF BEEF WITH SAUERKRAUT

Take about three pounds of fat, young beef (you may make soup stock of it first), then take out the bones, salt it well and lay it in the bottom of a kettle, put a quart of sauerkraut on top of it and let it boil slowly until tender. Add vinegar if necessary, thicken with a grated raw potato and add a little brown sugar. Some like a few caraway seeds added.

SAUERBRATEN

Take a piece of cross-rib or middle cut of chuck about three pounds, and put it in a deep earthen jar and pour enough boiling vinegar over it to cover; you may take one-third water. Add to the vinegar when boiling four bay leaves, some whole peppercorns, cloves and whole mace. Pour this over the meat and turn it daily. In summer three days is the longest time allowed for the meat to remain in this pickle; but in winter eight days is not too long. When ready to boil, heat one tablespoon drippings in a stew-pan. Cut up one or two onions in it; stew until tender and then put in the beef, salting it on both sides before stewing. Stew closely covered and if not acid enough add some of the brine in which it was pickled. Stew about three hours and thicken the gravy with flour.

ROLLED BEEF—POT-ROASTED

Take one pound and one-half of tenderloin, sprinkle it with parsley and onion; season with pepper and salt; roll and tie it. Place it in a pan with soup stock (or water if you have no stock), carrot and bay leaf and pot roast for one and one-half hours. Serve with tomato or brown sauce.

MOCK DUCK

Take the tenderloin, lay it flat on a board after removing the fat. Make a stuffing as for poultry. See "To Stuff Poultry". Spread this mixture on the meat evenly; then roll and tie it with white twine; turn in the ends to make it even and shapely.

Cut into dice an onion, turnip, and carrot, and place them in a baking-pan; lay the rolled meat on the bed of vegetables; pour in enough stock or water to cover the pan one inch deep; add a bouquet made of parsley, one bay leaf and three cloves; cover with another pan, and let cook slowly for four hours, basting frequently. It can be done in a pot just as well, and should be covered as tight as possible; when cooked, strain off the vegetables; thicken the gravy with one tablespoon of flour browned in fat and serve it with the meat. Long, slow cooking is required to make the meat tender. If cooked too fast it will not be good.

MARROWBONES

Have the bones cut into pieces two or three inches long; scrape and wash them very clean; spread a little thick dough on each end to keep the marrow in; then tie each bone in a piece of cloth and boil them for one hour. Remove the cloth and paste, and place each bone on a square of toast; sprinkle with red pepper and serve very hot. Or the marrow-bone can be boiled without being cut, the marrow then removed with a spoon and placed on squares of hot toast. Serve for luncheon.

ROAST BEEF, No. 1

Take prime rib roast. Cut up a small onion, a celery root and part of a carrot into rather small pieces and add to these two or three sprigs of parsley and one bay leaf. Sprinkle these over the bottom of the dripping-pan and place your roast on this bed. The oven should be very hot when the roast is first put in, but when the roast is browned sufficiently to retain its juices, moderate the heat and roast more slowly until the meat is done. Do not season until the roast is browned, and then add salt and pepper. Enough juice and fat will drop from the roast to give the necessary broth for basting. Baste frequently and turn occasionally, being very careful, however, not to stick a fork into the roast.

ROAST BEEF, No. 2

Season meat with salt and paprika. Dredge with flour. Place on rack in dripping-pan with two or three tablespoons fat, in hot oven, to brown quickly. Reduce heat and baste every ten minutes with the fat that has fried out. When meat is about half done, turn it over, dredge with flour, finish browning. If necessary, add a small quantity of water. Allow fifteen to twenty minutes for each pound of meat.

Three pounds is the smallest roast practicable.

ROAST BEEF (RUSSIAN STYLE)

Place a piece of cross-rib or shoulder weighing three pounds in roasting-pan, slice some onions over it, season with salt and pepper, add some water and let it cook well. Then peel a few potatoes and put them under the meat. When the meat becomes brown, turn it and cook until it browns on the other side.

WIENER BRATEN—VIENNA ROAST

Take a shoulder, have the bone taken out and then pound the meat well with a mallet. Lay it in vinegar for twenty-four hours. Heat some fat or goose oil in a deep pan or kettle which has a cover that fits air tight and lay the meat in the hot fat and sprinkle the upper side with salt, pepper and ginger. Put an onion in with the meat; stick about half a dozen cloves in the onion and add one bay leaf. Now turn the meat over and sprinkle the other side with salt, pepper and ginger. Cut up one or two tomatoes and pour some soup stock over all, and a dash of white wine. Cover closely and stew very slowly for three or four hours, turning the meat now and then; in doing so do not pierce with the fork, as this will allow the juice to escape. Do not add any water. Make enough potato pancakes to serve one or two to each person with "Wiener Braten."

TO BROIL STEAK BY GAS

Wipe steak with a damp cloth. Trim off the surplus fat. When the oven has been heated for from five to seven minutes, lay steak on a rack, greased, as near the flame as possible, the position of the rack depending on the thickness of the steak. Let the steak sear on each side, thereby retaining the juice. Then lower the rack somewhat, and allow the steak to broil to the degree required. Just before taking from the oven, salt and pepper and spread with melted chicken fat.

You can get just as good results in preparing chops and fish in the broiling oven.

BROILED BEEFSTEAK

Heat the gridiron, put in the steak, turn the gridiron over the hot coals at intervals of two minutes and then repeatedly at intervals of one minute. Sprinkle with salt and pepper, and serve on a hot platter.

Chops are done in the same way, but the gridiron is turned twice at intervals of two minutes and six times at intervals of one minute.

FRIED STEAK WITH ONIONS

Season the steak with salt and pepper, and dredge with flour. If tough, chop on both sides with a sharp knife. Lay in a pan of hot fat, when brown on one side, turn and brown on the other. While the steak is frying, heat some fat in another fryer and drop in four of five white onions that have been cut up. Fry crisp but not black. Remove the steak to a hot platter, stir one tablespoon of flour in the fryer until smooth, add one-half cup of boiling water. Lay the crisp onions over the steak, then over all pour the brown gravy.

FRIED BEEFSTEAK

Take third cut of chuck or the tenderloin. Have the spider very hot, use just enough fat to grease the spider. Lay in the steak, turning very often to keep in the juice, season with salt and pepper. Serve on a hot platter.

BRUNSWICK STEW

Cook one pound of brisket of beef and three pounds of young chicken with one pint of soup stock or water, one pint of Lima beans, four ears of cut corn (cut from cob), three potatoes diced, two tomatoes quartered; one small onion, one teaspoon of paprika and one teaspoon of salt. Let all these simmer until tender, and before serving remove the meat and any visible chicken bones.

This stew may be made of breast of veal omitting the chicken and brisket.

BREAST FLANK (SHORT RIBS) AND YELLOW TURNIPS

Get the small ribs and put on with plenty of water, an onion, pepper and salt. After boiling about one and one-half hours add a large yellow turnip cut in small pieces; one-half hour before serving add six potatoes cut in small pieces. Water must be added as necessary. A little sugar will improve flavor, and as it simmers the turnip will soften and give the whole dish the appearance of a stew.

MEAT OLIVES

Have a flank steak cut in three inch squares. Spread each piece with the following dressing: one cup of bread crumbs, two tablespoons of minced parsley; one chopped onion, a dash of red pepper and one teaspoon of salt. Moisten with one-fourth cup of melted fat. Roll up and tie in shape. Cover with water and simmer until meat is tender. Take the olives from the sauce and brown in the oven. Thicken the sauce with one-fourth cup of flour moistened with water to form a thin paste.

SHORT RIB OF BEEF, SPANISH

Get the small ribs of beef and put on with water enough to cover, seasoning with salt, pepper, an onion and a tiny clove of garlic. Let it cook about two hours, then add a can of tomatoes and season highly either with red peppers or paprika. Cook at least three hours.

BRAISED OXTAILS

Two oxtails, jointed and washed; six onions sliced and browned in pot with oxtails. When nicely browned add water enough to cover and stew slowly one hour; then add two carrots, if small; one green pepper, sprig of parsley, one-half cup of tomatoes and six small potatoes, and cook until tender. Thicken with browned flour. Cook separately eight lengths of macaroni; place cooked macaroni on dish and pour ragout over it and serve hot.

To brown flour take one-half cup of flour, put in pan over moderate heat and stir until nicely browned.

HUNGARIAN GOULASH

Have two pounds of beef cut into one inch squares. Dredge in flour and fry until brown. Cover with water and simmer for two hours; the last half-hour add one tablespoon of salt and one-eighth of a teaspoon of pepper. Make a sauce by cooking one cup of tomatoes and one stalk of celery cut in small pieces, a bay leaf and two whole cloves, for twenty-five minutes; rub through a sieve, add to stock in which meat was cooked. Thicken with four tablespoons of flour moistened with two tablespoons of water. Serve meat with cooked diced potatoes, carrots, and green and red peppers cut in strips.

RUSSIAN GOULASH

To one pound beef, free from fat and cut up as pan stew, add one chopped green pepper, one large onion, two blades of garlic (cut fine), pepper and salt, with just enough water to cover. Let this simmer until meat is very tender. Add a little water as needed. Put in medium sized can of tomatoes an hour or so before using and have ready two cups of cooked spaghetti or macaroni and put this into the meat until thoroughly heated. This must not be too wet; let water cook away just before adding the tomatoes.

BEEF LOAF

To two pounds of chopped beef take three egg yolks, three tablespoons of parsley, three tablespoons of melted chicken-fat, four heaping tablespoons of soft bread crumbs, one-half teaspoon of kitchen bouquet, two teaspoons of lemon juice, grated peel of one lemon, one teaspoon of salt, one-half teaspoon of onion-juice and one teaspoon of pepper. Mix and bake twenty-five minutes in a quick oven with one-fourth cup of melted chicken-fat, and one-half cup of boiling water. Baste often.

HAMBURGER STEAK

Take one pound of raw beef, cut off fat and stringy pieces, chop extremely fine, season with salt and pepper, grate in part of an onion or fry with onions. Make into round cakes a little less than one-half inch thick. Heat pan blue hot, grease lightly; add cakes, count sixty, then turn them and cook on the other side until brown. When well browned they are done if liked rare. Cook ten minutes if liked well done.

BITKI (RUSSIAN HAMBURGER STEAK)

Take two cups of clear beef chopped, and two cups of bread crumbs that have been soaked in a little water, leaving them quite moist, mix thoroughly with the beef, season with pepper and salt and shape into individual cakes. Fry as directed for Hamburger Steak.

CHOPPED MEAT WITH RAISINS (ROUMANIAN)

Take a pound of chopped meat, add grated onion, an egg, matzoth flour, white pepper, mix and form into small balls, put in pot with one-half cup of water, fat, sugar, a quarter cup of large black raisins, a few slices of lemon and let stew one-half hour, then thicken gravy with tablespoon of flour browned in a tablespoon of fat and serve.

CARNATZLICH (ROUMANIAN)

One pound of tenderloin, chopped, add an egg, a little paprika, black pepper, salt and four cloves of garlic (which have been scraped, and let stand in a little salt for ten minutes, and then mashed so it looks like dough). Form this meat mixture into short sausage-like rolls; boil one-half hour and serve at once.

Serve this dish with Slaitta. (See Vegetables.)

BAKED HASH

Mix together one cup of chopped meat, one cup of cold mashed potatoes, one-half an onion, minced, one well-beaten egg and one-half cup of soup stock. Season rather highly with salt, if unsalted meat is used, paprika and celery salt, turn into greased baking dish and bake for twenty minutes in a well-heated oven. The same mixture may be fried, but will not taste as good.

SOUP MEAT

The meat must be cooked until very tender then lift it out of the soup and lay upon a platter and season while hot. Heat a tablespoon of fat or drippings of roast beef in a spider, cut up a few slices of onion in it, also half a clove of garlic, add a tablespoon of flour, stirring all the time; then add soup stock or rich gravy, and the soup meat, which has been seasoned with salt, pepper and ginger. You must sprinkle the spices on both sides of the meat, and add one-half teaspoon of caraway seed to the sauce, and if too thick add more soup stock and a little boiling water. Cover closely and let it simmer about fifteen minutes.

LEFT-OVER MEAT

There are many ways to utilize left-over meat.

Indeed, not one particle of meat should ever be wasted.

Cold roasts of beef, lamb, mutton or any cold joint roasted or boiled may be made into soups, stews, minces or used for sandwiches, or just served cold with vegetables or salads.

SPAGHETTI AND MEAT

Break spaghetti in small pieces and boil until tender. Put left-over meat through chopper and mix with the spaghetti, salt, pepper, and a little onion juice. Grease a baking dish and put in the meat and spaghetti, sprinkle on top with bread crumbs and bake in a moderate oven.

MEAT PIE

Cut any left-over beef, lamb or veal in small pieces, removing all excess of fat; parboil one green pepper (seeds removed) cut in strips, two cups of potatoes and one-half cup of carrots cut in dice, and one onion chopped fine. Add to the meat. Thicken with one-fourth cup of flour moistened in cold water. Put in a baking dish. The crust is made as follows: One cup of flour, one heaping teaspoon of drippings, pinch of salt, one-fourth teaspoon of baking powder, one teaspoon of sugar and cold water to mix, about one-third cup. Roll out to fit baking dish, cut holes for steam to escape, after covering the contents of the dish. Bake in a quick hot oven one-half hour.

PICKLED MEAT—HOME-MADE CORNED BEEF

Take four quarts of water, adding enough salt to float an egg, boil this salted water, when cool take four or five pounds brisket of beef, seasoned with whole and ground peppers, one large clove of garlic, pierced in different parts of the beef, one tablespoon of sugar, one bay leaf and one teaspoon of saltpetre. Put meat into deep stone pot, pour the boiled water over it and store in a cool place for ten days or two weeks.

BOILED CORNED BEEF

Put corned beef into cold water; using enough to cover it well; let it come slowly to the boiling-point; then place where it will simmer only; allow thirty minutes or more to each pound. It is improved by adding a few soup vegetables the last hour of cooking.

If the piece can be used a second time, trim it to good shape; place it again in the water in which it was boiled; let it get heated through; then set aside to cool in the water, and under pressure, a plate or deep dish holding a flat-iron being set on top of the meat. The water need not rise above the meat sufficiently to wet the iron. When cooled under pressure the meat is more firm and cuts better into slices.

Cabbage is usually served with hot corned beef, but should not be boiled with it.

ENCHILADAS

Make a dough of cornmeal and wheat flour and water. Roll it out in thin, round cakes; cook quickly in a pan that has not been greased, then roll in a cloth to keep soft and warm. Grind one cup of sausage, add one-half grated onion, one tablespoon of Worcestershire sauce, and fill the warm cakes with this mixture. Roll them when filled, and pour over them a sauce made of two tablespoons of drippings into which two tablespoons of flour have been smoothed. Add one cup of soup stock, one cup of strained tomatoes, two tablespoons of vinegar, one tablespoon of Spanish pepper sauce.

VIENNA SAUSAGE

Wash and put on in boiling water. Boil ten minutes, fill a deep dish with hot water, put sausages in, cover, and serve in hot water. To be eaten with grated horseradish or French mustard.

SMOKED BEEF

Soak overnight in cold water; next morning place it in cold water, and simmer till quite tender, reckoning one-half hour to the pound.

ROAST VEAL

The shoulder and breast of veal are best for roasting. Always buy veal that is fat and white. Prepare for the oven in the following manner: Wash and then dry; rub it well with salt, a very little ground ginger, and dredge it well with flour. Lay in roasting-pan and put slices of onion on top with a few tablespoons of goose-fat or drippings. Cover tightly and roast, allowing twenty minutes to the pound and baste frequently. Veal must be well done. When cold it slices up as nicely as turkey.

BREAST OF VEAL—ROASTED

Roast as directed above. Have the butcher cut a pocket to receive the stuffing. Prepare bread stuffing and sew up the pocket. Sprinkle a little caraway seed on top of the roast. A tablespoon of lemon juice adds to the flavor. Baste often.

STEWED VEAL

Prepare as above, but do not have the meat cut in small pieces. If desired one-half teaspoon of caraway seed may be used instead of the parsley. Mashed potatoes and green peas or stewed tomatoes are usually served with veal.

Any of the flour or potato dumplings are excellent served with stewed or fricasseed veal.

FRICASSEED VEAL WITH CAULIFLOWER

Use the breast or shoulder for this purpose, the former being preferable, and cut it up into pieces, not too small. Sprinkle each piece slightly with fine salt and ginger. Heat a tablespoon of goose-oil or poultry drippings in a stew-pan, and lay the veal in it. Cut up an onion and one or two tomatoes (a tablespoon of canned tomatoes will do), and add to this a little water, and stew two hours, closely covered. When done mix a teaspoon of flour and a little water and add to the veal. Chop up a few sprigs of parsley, add it and boil up once and serve. Place the cauliflower around the platter in which you serve the veal. Boil the cauliflower in salt and water, closely covered.

STUFFED SHOULDER OF VEAL

Have the blade removed, and fill the space with a stuffing made of bread crumbs, thyme, lemon juice, salt, pepper to taste and one egg, also chopped mushrooms if desired. Sew up the opening, press and tie it into good shape and roast. The stuffing may be made of minced meat, cut from the veal, and highly seasoned.

VEAL LOAF

Take two pounds of chopped veal, four tablespoons of bread crumbs, two beaten eggs, season with salt, pepper, ginger, nutmeg and a little water. Add a tablespoon of chicken-fat; grease the pan, mix ingredients thoroughly, form into a loaf, spread or lay piece of chicken-fat on top. Bake in oblong tin until done, basting frequently.

POULTRY

TO DRESS AND CLEAN POULTRY

Singe by holding the fowl over a flame from gas, alcohol or burning paper. Pick off pin feathers. Cut off the nails, then cut off the head, turn back the skin and cut the neck off quite close; take out windpipe and crop, cutting off close to the body. Cut through the skin around the leg one inch below the leg joint; take out the tendons and break the leg at the joint; in old birds each tendon must be removed separately by using a skewer.

Make an incision just below the breast bone large enough to insert your hand, take out the fat and loosen the entrails with your forefinger. When everything is removed, cut off the wings close to the body, also the neck, feet and head. Separate the gall from the liver. In doing this be very careful not to break the gall, which has a very thin skin. Scrape all the fat off carefully that adheres to the entrails and lay it in a separate dish of water overnight. Cut open the gizzard, clean and pull off the skin, or inner lining.

Make Kosher as directed in "Rules for Kashering".

If you make use of the head, which you may in soup, cut off the top of the bill, split open the head, lengthwise, take out the brains, eyes and tongue.

Clean the gizzard and feet by laying them in scalding water for a few moments, this will loosen the skin, which can then be easily removed.

Remove the oil bag from the upper side of tail.

After making Kosher and cleaning poultry, season all fowls for several hours before cooking. Salt, pepper, and ginger are the proper seasoning. Some like a tiny bit of garlic rubbed inside and outside, especially for goose or duck.

Dress and clean goose, duck, squab, and turkey as directed for chicken.

TO TRUSS A CHICKEN

Press the thighs and wings close against the body; fasten securely with skewers and tie with string. Draw the skin of the neck to the back and fasten it.

ROAST CHICKEN

Stuff and truss a chicken, season with pepper and salt and dredge with flour. Put in a roasting-pan with two or three tablespoons of chicken-fat if the chicken is not especially fat. When heated add hot water and baste frequently. The oven should be hot and the time necessary for a large chicken will be about an hour and a half. When done, remove the chicken, pour off the grease and make a brown sauce in the pan.

CHICKEN CASSEROLE

Bake chicken in covered casserole until nearly tender, then add three potatoes cut in dice; boil small pieces of carrots, green peas, and small white onions—each to be boiled separately. Just before serving, thicken gravy with a teaspoon of flour mixed with a half cup of soup stock or water. Season to taste and place vegetables around the dish.

BOILED CHICKEN, BAKED

Make chicken soup with an old hen. Remove chicken from soup just as soon as tender. Place in roasting-pan with three tablespoons of chicken-fat, one onion sliced, one clove of garlic, one-half teaspoon each of salt and paprika. Sprinkle with soft bread crumbs. Baste frequently and when sufficiently browned, cut in pieces for serving. Place on platter with the strained gravy pour over the chicken and serve.

BROILED SPRING CHICKEN

Take young spring chickens of one to one and one-half pounds in weight, and split down the back, break the joints and remove the breast bone. Sprinkle with salt and pepper and rub well with chicken-fat. Place in broiler and broil twenty minutes over a clear fire, or under the flame in broiling oven of gas stove, being careful to turn broiler that all parts may be equally browned. The flesh side must be exposed to the fire the greater part of the time as the skin side will brown quickly. Remove to hot platter.

Or chicken may be placed in dripping pan, skin side down, seasoned with salt and pepper and spread with chicken-fat, and bake fifteen minutes in a hot oven and then broiled to finish.

Serve with giblet sauce.

FRIED SPRING CHICKEN

Cut it up as for fricassee and see that every piece is wiped dry. Have ready heated in a spider some goose-fat or other poultry drippings. Season each piece of chicken with salt and ground ginger, or pepper. Roll each piece of chicken in sifted cracker or bread crumbs (which you have previously seasoned with salt). Fry in the spider, turning often, and browning evenly. You may cut up some parsley and add while frying. If the chicken is quite large, it is better to steam it before frying.

GIBLETS

Heart, liver and gizzard constitute the giblets, and to these the neck is usually added. Wash them; put them in cold water and cook until tender. This will take several hours. Serve with the chicken; or mash the liver, mince the heart and gizzard and add them to the brown sauce. Save the stock in which they are cooked for making the sauce.

CHICKEN FRICASSEE

Take a chicken, cut off the wings, legs and neck. Separate the breast from the chicken, leaving it whole. Cut the back into two pieces. Prepare a mixture of salt, ginger and a little pepper in a saucer and dust each piece of chicken with this mixture. When you are ready to cook the chicken, take all the particles of fat you have removed from it and lay in the bottom of the kettle, also a small onion, cut up, some parsley root and celery. Lay the chicken upon this, breast first, then the leg and so on. Cover up tight and let it stew slowly on the back of the stove (or over a low gas flame), adding hot water when necessary. Just before serving chop up some parsley, fine, and rub a teaspoon of flour in a little cold water, and add. Let it boil up once. Shake the kettle back and forth to prevent becoming lumpy. The parsley root and celery may be omitted if so desired.

Duck can be prepared in this manner.

CHICKEN WITH RICE

Joint a chicken; season with salt and ground ginger and boil with water enough to cover. Allow one-half pound of rice to one chicken. Boil this after chicken is tender. Serve together on a large platter.

CHICKEN (TURKISH STYLE)

Brown a chicken, cover with water and season, cook until tender. When chicken is tender; slash the skin of chestnuts, put them in oven and roast, then skin them, put in chicken and let come to a boil and serve with the chicken.

AMASTICH

Cook one pound of rice in a quart of stock for half an hour, stirring frequently. Then add a chicken stuffed and trussed as for roasting; cover closely and cook thoroughly. After removing the chicken, pass the liquor through a strainer, add the juice of a lemon and the beaten yolk of an egg, and pour over the bird.

CHICKEN WITH SPAGHETTI EN CASSEROLE

Prepare and truss a young chicken, as if for roasting. Put it in a casserole; and pour over it two tablespoons of olive oil, a cup of white wine, a cup of bouillon, salt and cayenne to taste, one spoon of dried mushrooms soaked in one cup of water and chopped fine, and one-half can of mushrooms. Cover tightly and simmer in the oven for about an hour, turning the chicken occasionally; add a dozen olives and a tablespoon of chicken-fat, smoothed with one tablespoon of flour, and bring to a boil. Remove the chicken and add about a pint of boiled spaghetti to the sauce. Place the chicken on a platter, surround with the spaghetti, and serve.

STUFFED CHICKEN (TURKISH STYLE)

Steam chicken and when it is almost tender stuff it with the following: Take one-fourth pound of almonds, chopped; season with parsley, pepper and salt to taste, add one tablespoon of bread crumbs and bind this with one well-beaten egg. Put chicken in roasting-pan and roast until done.

SMOTHERED CHICKEN

Two tender chickens cut in half, split down the back; place the pieces in a colander to drain well, after having been well salted; season with pepper; grease well the bottom of a baking-pan; add one stalk finely chopped celery, onion; lay the chicken on breast, side up; sprinkle lightly with flour, fat; two cups of hot water. Have the oven very hot when putting chickens in. As soon as browned evenly, cover with a pan, fitting closely. Reduce the heat of the oven; allow to cook slowly an hour or so longer, until tender. Place on a hot platter; set in oven until sauce is made, as follows: put the pan on top of stove in which chickens were smothered; add level tablespoon of flour, thinned in cold water; add minced parsley; let this all cook two or three minutes, then add large cup of strong stock, to the chickens. Broil one can mushrooms, and pour these over chicken when ready to serve.

CHICKEN CURRY

Cut chickens in pieces for serving; dredge in flour and sauté in hot fat. Cut one onion in thin pieces, add one tablespoon of curry powder, three-fourths of a tablespoon of salt and one tablespoon of wine vinegar. Add to chicken, cover with boiling water; simmer until chicken is tender. Thicken sauce and serve with steamed rice.

CHICKEN PAPRIKA WITH RICE

Cut a three and one-half pound fat chicken in pieces to serve, salt it and let stand several hours. Heat one-fourth cup of fat in an iron kettle, add one medium-sized onion, minced; fry golden brown and set aside. Fry the chicken in the fat and when nicely browned, add paprika to taste and boiling water to cover, and let simmer one hour.

Soak one cup of rice in cold water, drain, add the fried onion and one teaspoon of salt and gradually three cups of chicken broth, more if necessary. When nearly done add the chicken and finish cooking in a slow oven, one-half hour.

CHILI CON CARNE

Cut two broilers in pieces for serving. Season with salt, pepper, and dredge in flour; brown in hot fat. Parboil six large red peppers until soft, rub through a wire sieve. Chop two small onions fine, three cloves of garlic and one-fourth cup of capers. Combine, add to chicken, cover with water and cook until chicken is tender. Thicken the sauce with fat and flour melted together.

PILAF (RUSSIAN STYLE)

Follow recipe below but substitute cooked lamb for the chicken, and add chicken livers fried and cut in small pieces.

PILAF (TURKISH STYLE)

Soak one cup of rice in cold water for one hour. Pour off the water, and put the rice with two cups of soup stock and one-quarter of a white onion on to boil. Stew until the rice absorbs all the stock. Stew one-half can of tomatoes thoroughly and season with olive oil or chicken-fat, salt and pepper. Mix it with the rice.

Sauté in chicken-fat to a light color, a jointed chicken slightly parboiled, or slices of cold cooked chicken or turkey. Make a depression in the rice and tomato, put in the chicken and two tablespoons of olive oil or chicken-fat, and stew all together for twenty minutes. Serve on a platter in a smooth mound, the red rice surrounding the fowl.

SPANISH PIE

Take one pint of cold chicken, duck or any poultry. Cut it into flakes and place it in a pudding dish which has been lined with a thin crust. On the layer of meat place a layer of sweet red peppers (seeds removed), cut in slices; next, a layer of thinly sliced sausage, and so on until the dish is full. Over this pour a glass of claret into which have been rubbed two tablespoons of flour. Cover with a thin crust of pastry, and bake.

CHICKEN À LA ITALIENNE

Cut the remains of cold chicken (or turkey) into pieces about an inch long and marinate them in a bowl containing one tablespoon of olive oil; one teaspoon of tarragon vinegar or lemon juice, a few drops of onion juice, salt and pepper. At the end of half an hour sprinkle with finely chopped parsley, dip them in fritter batter, and fry in boiling fat. Drain on a brown paper, and serve with or without tomato or brown sauce.

In some parts of Italy this dish is made of several kinds of cold meats, poultry, brains, etc. (the greater the variety the better), served on the same platter, and in Spain all kinds of cold vegetables are fried in batter and served together.

ROAST GOOSE

All goose meat tastes better if it is well rubbed with salt, ginger and a little garlic a day previous to using.

Stuff goose with bread dressing, or chestnut dressing, a dressing of apples is also very good. (See "Stuffings for Meat and Poultry".) Sew up the goose, then line a sheet-iron roasting-pan with a few slices of onion and celery and place the goose upon these, cover closely, roast three hours or more, according to weight. If the goose browns too quickly, cover with greased paper or lower the heat of the oven. Baste every fifteen minutes.

GESCHUNDENE GANS

Take a very fat goose for this purpose. After cleaning and singeing, cut off neck, wings and feet. Lay the goose on a table, back up, take a sharp knife, make a cut from the neck down to the tai. Begin again at the top near the neck, take off the skin, holding it in your left hand, your knife in your right hand, after all the skin is removed, place it in cold water; separate the breast from back and cut off joints. Have ready in a plate a mixture of salt, ginger and a little garlic or onion, cut up fine. Rub the joints and small pieces with this, and make a small incision in each leg and four in the breast. Put in each incision a small piece of garlic or onion, and rub also with a prepared mixture of salt and ginger. Put away in stone jar overnight or until you wish to use.

GAENSEKLEIN

Rub wings, neck, gizzard, heart and back of goose with salt, ginger, pepper and garlic and set on the fire in a stew-pan with cold water. Cover tightly and stew slowly but steadily for four hours. When done skim off all the fat. Now put a spider over the fire, put into it about two or three tablespoons of the fat that you have just skimmed off and then add the fat to the meat again. Cut up fine a very small piece of garlic and add a heaping teaspoon of flour (brown). Add the hot gravy and pour all over the goose. Cover up tightly and set on back of stove till you wish to serve. You may cook the whole goose in this way after it is cut up.

STUFFED GOOSE NECK (RUSSIAN STYLE)

Remove skin from neck of goose, duck or chicken in one piece. Wash and clean well and stuff with same mixture as for Kischtke. Sew at both ends and roast in hot oven until well browned.

STUFFED GOOSE NECK

Remove the fat skin from the neck of a fat goose, being careful not to put any holes in it. Clean carefully and sew up the smaller end and stuff through larger end with the following:

Grind fine some pieces of raw goose meat (taken from the breast or legs), grind also some soft or "linda fat" a thin piece of garlic, a small piece of onion, when fine add one egg and a little soaked bread, season with salt, pepper, and ginger. When neck is stuffed, sew up larger end, lay it in a pudding-pan, pour a little cold water over it, set in stove and baste from time to time. Let brown until crisp. Eat hot.

GOOSE CRACKLINGS (GRIEBEN)

Cut the thick fat of a fat goose in pieces as big as the palm of your hand, roll together and run a toothpick through each one to fasten. Put a large preserve kettle on top of hot stove, lay in the cracklings, sprinkle a tiny bit of salt over them and pour in a cup or two of cold water; cover closely and let cook not too fast, until water is cooked out. Then add the soft or "linda" fat, keep top off and let all brown nicely. About one to two hours is required to cook them. If you do not wish the scraps of "Greben" brittle, take them out of the fat before they are browned. Place strainer over your fat crock, to catch the clear fat and let greben drain. If greben are too greasy place in baking-pan in oven a few minutes to try out a little more. Serve at lunch with rye bread.

ROAST GOOSE BREASTS

The best way to roast a goose breast is to remove the skin from the neck and sew it over the breast and fasten it with a few stitches under the breast, making an incision with a pointed knife in the breast and joints of the goose, so as to be able to insert a little garlic (or onion) in each incision, also a little salt and ginger. Keep closely covered all the time, so as not to get too brown. They cut up nicely cold for sandwiches.

GOOSE MEAT, PRESERVED IN FAT

If too fat to roast, render the fat of goose, remove and cut the skin into small pieces. The scraps, when brown, shriveled and crisp, are then "Greben," and are served hot or cold. When fat is nearly done or clear, add the breast and legs of goose, previously salted, and boil in the fat until tender and browned. Place meat in crock and pour the clear, hot fat over it to cover. Cool. Cover crock with plate and stone and keep in a cool, dry place. Will keep for months. When ready to serve, take out meat, heat, and drain off fat.

SMOKED GOOSE BREAST

Dried or smoked goose breast must be prepared in the following manner: Take the breast of a fat goose; leave the skin on; rub well with salt, pepper and saltpetre; pack in a stone jar and let it remain pickled thus four or five days. Dry well, cover with gauze and send away to be smoked.

SMOKED GOOSE

Remove skin. Place legs, neck and skin of neck of geschundene goose (fat goose) to one side. Scrape the meat carefully from the bones, neck, back, etc., of the goose, remove all tendons and tissues and chop very fine. Fill this in the skin of the neck and sew up with coarse thread on both ends. Rub the filled neck, the legs and the breast with plenty of garlic (sprinkle with three-eighths pound of salt and one tablespoon of sugar and one teaspoon of saltpetre), and enough water to form a brine. Place the neck, legs and breast in a stone jar, cover with a cloth and put weights on top. Put aside for seven days, turn once in a while. Take out of the brine, cover with gauze and send to the butcher to smoke. When done, serve cold, sliced thin.

STEWED GOOSE, PIQUANTE

Cut up, after being skinned, and stew, seasoning with salt, pepper, a few cloves and a very little lemon peel. When done heat a little goose fat in a frying-pan, brown half a tablespoon of flour, add a little vinegar and the juice of half a lemon.

MINCED GOOSE (HUNGARIAN STYLE)

Take the entire breast of a goose, chop up fine in a chopping bowl; grate in part of an onion, and season with salt, pepper and a tiny piece of garlic. Add some grated stale bread and work in a few eggs. Press this chopped meat back on to the breast bone and roast, basting very often with goose fat.

DUCK

Singe off all the small feathers; cut off neck and wings, which may be used for soup; wash thoroughly and rub well with salt, ginger and a little pepper, inside and out. Now prepare this dressing: Take the liver, gizzard and heart and chop to a powder in chopping bowl. Grate in a little nutmeg, add a piece of celery root and half an onion. Put all this into your chopping bowl. Soak some stale bread, squeeze out all the water and fry in a spider of hot fat. Toss this soaked bread into the bowl; add one egg, salt, pepper and a speck of ginger and mix all thoroughly. Fill the duck with this and sew it up. Lay in the roasting-pan with slices of onions, celery and specks of fat. Put some on top of fowl; roast two hours, covered up tight and baste often. Stick a fork into the skin from time to time so that the fat will try out.

ROAST DUCK

Draw the duck; stuff, truss and roast the same as chicken. Serve with giblet sauce and currant jelly. If small, the duck should be cooked in an hour.

DUCK À LA MODE IN JELLY

One duckling of about five pounds, one calf's foot, eight to ten small onions, as many young carrots, one bunch of parsley. Cook the foot slowly in one quart of water, one teaspoon of salt and a small bay leaf. Put aside when the liquor has been reduced to one-half. In the meanwhile fry the duck and when well browned wipe off the grease, put in another pan, add the calf's foot with its broth, one glass of dry white wine, a tablespoon of brandy, the carrots, parsley and the onions—the latter slightly browned in drippings—pepper and salt to taste and cook slowly under a covered lid for one hour. Cool off for about an hour, take off the grease, bone and skin the duckling and cut the meat into small pieces; arrange nicely with the vegetables in individual earthenware dishes, cover with the stock and put on the ice to harden.

SQUABS, OR NEST PIGEONS

Pick, singe, draw, clean and season them well inside and out, with salt mixed with a little ginger and pepper, and then stuff them with well-seasoned bread dressing. Pack them closely in a deep stew-pan and cover with flakes of goose fat, minced parsley and a little chopped onion. Cover with a lid that fits close and stew gently, adding water when necessary. Do not let them get too brown. They should be a light yellow.

BROILED SQUABS

Squabs are a great delicacy, especially in the convalescent's menu, being peculiarly savory and nourishing. Clean the squabs; lay them in salt water for about ten minutes and then rub dry with a clean towel. Split them down the back and broil over a clear coal fire. Season with salt and pepper; lay them on a heated platter, grease them liberally with goose fat and cover with a deep platter. Toast a piece of bread for each pigeon, removing the crust. Dip the toast in boiling water for an instant. In serving lay a squab upon a piece of toasted bread.

PIGEON PIE

Prepare as many pigeons as you wish to bake in your pie. Salt and pepper, then melt some fat in a stew-pan, and cut up an onion in it. When hot, place in the pigeons and stew until tender. In the meantime line a deep pie plate with a rich paste. Cut up the pigeons, lay them in, with hard-boiled eggs chopped up and minced parsley. Season with salt and pepper. Put flakes of chicken fat rolled in flour here and there, pour over the gravy the pigeons were stewed in, cover with a crust. Bake slowly until done.

SQUAB EN CASSEROLE

Take fowl and brown in a skillet the desired color, then add to this enough water (or soup stock preferred), put it in casserole and add vegetables; add first those that require longest cooking. Use mushrooms, carrots, small potatoes and peas. If you like flavor of sherry wine, add small wine glass; if not, it is just as good. Season well and cook in hot oven not too long, as you want fowl and vegetables to be whole. You may add soup stock if it is too dry after being in oven.

ROAST TURKEY

Singe and clean the turkey the same as chicken. Fill with plain bread stuffing or chestnut stuffing. Tie down the legs and rub entire surface with salt and let stand overnight. Next morning place in large drippings or roasting-pan on rack and spread breast, legs and wings with one-third cup of fat creamed and mixed with one-fourth cup of flour. Dredge bottom of pan with flour. Place in a hot oven and when the flour on the turkey begins to brown, reduce the heat and add two cups of boiling water or the stock in which the giblets are cooking, and baste with one-fourth cup of fat and three-fourths cup of boiling water. When this is all used, baste with the fat in the pan. Baste every fifteen minutes until tender; do not prick with a fork, press with the fingers; if the breast meat and leg are soft to the touch the turkey is done. If the oven is too hot, cover the pan; turn the turkey often, that it may brown nicely. Remove strings and skewers and serve on hot platter. Serve with giblet sauce and cranberry sauce. If the turkey is very large it will require three hours or more, a small one will require only an hour and a half.

STUFFED TURKEY NECK (TURKISH STYLE)

Take neck of turkey, stuff with following: One-quarter pound of almonds or walnuts chopped fine and seasoned with chopped parsley, pepper and salt, put two hard-boiled eggs in the centre of this dressing; stuff neck, sew up the ends and when roasted slice across so as to have a portion of the hard-boiled egg on each slice; place on platter and surround with sprigs of parsley.

STUFFINGS FOR MEAT AND POULTRY

TO STUFF POULTRY

Use enough stuffing to fill the bird but do not pack it tightly or the stuffing will be soggy. Close the small openings with a skewer; sew the larger one with linen thread and a long needle. Remove skewers and strings before serving.

CRUMB DRESSING

Take one tablespoon of chicken fat, mix in two cups of bread crumbs, pinch of salt and pepper, a few drops of onion juice, one tablespoon of chopped parsley, and lastly one well-beaten egg. Mix all on stove in skillet, remove from fire and stuff fowl.

BREAD DRESSING FOR FOWL

In a fryer on the stove heat two tablespoons of drippings or fat, drop in one-half onion cut fine, brown lightly and add one-quarter loaf of stale baker's bread (which has previously been soaked in cold water and then thoroughly squeezed out). Cook until it leaves the sides of the fryer, stirring occasionally. If too dry add a little soup stock. Remove from the fire, put in a bowl, season with salt, pepper, ginger, and finely chopped parsley, add a small lump of fat, break in one whole egg, mix well and fill the fowl with it.

MEAT DRESSING FOR POULTRY

If you cannot buy sausage meat at your butcher's have him chop some for you, adding a little fat. Also mix in some veal with the beef while chopping. Season with salt, pepper, nutmeg or thyme. Grate in a piece of celery root and a piece of garlic about the size of a bean, add a small onion, a minced tomato, a quarter of a loaf of stale bread; also grated, and mix up the whole with one egg. If you prefer, you may soak the bread, press out every drop of water and dry in a heated spider with fat.

POTATO STUFFING

Add two cups of hot, mashed Irish or sweet potatoes to bread stuffing. Mix well and stuff in goose, stuffed veal or lamb breast, or in beef casings, cleaned and dressed.

CHESTNUT STUFFING

Shell and blanch two cups of chestnuts. Cook in boiling salted water until tender. Drain and force through a colander or a potato ricer. Add one-fourth cup of melted chicken fat, one-fourth teaspoon of pepper, three-fourths of a teaspoon of salt, one cup of grated bread crumbs, and enough soup stock to moisten.

RAISIN STUFFING

Take three cups of stale bread crumbs; add one-half a cup of melted chicken fat, one cup of seeded raisins cut in small pieces, one teaspoon of salt and one-fourth teaspoon of white pepper. Mix thoroughly.

VEGETABLES

All vegetables should be thoroughly cleansed just before being put on to cook.

Green vegetables; such as cabbage, cauliflower and Brussels sprouts, should be soaked heads down in salted cold water, to which a few spoons of vinegar may be added.

To secure the best results all vegetables except beans, that is the dried beans, should be put in boiling water and the water must be made to boil again as soon as possible after the vegetables have been added and must be kept boiling until the cooking is finished.

In cooking vegetables, conserve their juices.

The average housewife pours down the sink drainpipe the juices from all the vegetables which she cooks; she little realizes that she thus drains away the health of her family. Cook vegetables with just sufficient water to prevent them from burning, and serve their juices with them; else save the vegetable "waters" and, by the addition of milk and butter convert them into soups for the family use. Such soups, derived from one or several vegetables, alone or mixed together, make palatable and healthful additions to the family bill-of-fare.

ASPARAGUS

Cut off the woody part, scrape the lower part of the stalks. Wash well and tie in bunches. Put into a deep stew-pan, with the cut end resting on the bottom of the stew-pan. Pour in boiling water to come up to the tender heads, but not to cover them. Add one teaspoon of salt for each quart of water. Place where the water will boil. Cook until tender, having the cover partially off the stew-pan. This will be from fifteen to thirty minutes, depending upon the freshness and tenderness of the vegetable. Have some slices of well-toasted bread on a platter. Butter them slightly. Arrange the cooked asparagus on the toast, season with butter and a little salt and serve at once. Save the water in which the asparagus was boiled to use in making vegetable soup.

CANNED ASPARAGUS

Open one end of the can, as indicated on wrapper, so tips will be at opening. Pour off the liquid and allow cold water to run over gently and to rinse. Drain and pour boiling water over them in the can and set in a hot oven to heat thoroughly. When ready to serve, drain and arrange carefully on hot platter and serve same as fresh asparagus, hot on toast or cold with salad dressing, or with "Sauce Hollandaise", poured over.

ARTICHOKES (FRENCH OR GLOBE)

French artichokes have a large scaly head, like the cone of a pine tree.
The flower buds are used before they open.

The edible portion consists of the thickened portion at the base of the scales and the receptacle to which the leaf-like scales are attached.

When the artichoke is very young and tender the edible parts may be eaten raw as a salad. When it becomes hard, as it does very quickly, it must be cooked. When boiled it may be eaten as a salad or with a sauce. The scales are pulled with the fingers from the cooked head, the base of each leaf dipped in a sauce and then eaten.

The bottoms (receptacles), which many consider the most delicate part of the artichoke, may be cut up and served as a salad, or they may be stewed and served with a sauce. To prepare the artichoke remove all the hard outer leaves. Cut off the stem close to the leaves. Cut off the top of the bud. Drop the artichokes into boiling water and cook until tender, which will take from thirty to fifty minutes, then take up and remove the choke. Serve a dish of French salad dressing with the artichokes, which may be eaten either hot or cold. Melted butter also makes a delicious sauce for the artichokes if they are eaten hot.

JERUSALEM ARTICHOKE

This vegetable is in season in the fall and spring, and may be cooked like kohl-rabi and served in a white cream or sauce. The artichoke may also be cooked in milk.

When this is done, cut the washed and peeled artichoke into cubes, put in a stew-pan, and cover with milk (a generous pint to a quart of cubes). Add one small onion and cook twenty minutes. Beat together one tablespoon of butter and one level tablespoon of flour, and stir this into the boiling milk. Then season with one teaspoon of salt and one-fourth teaspoon of pepper, and continue the cooking one-half hour longer. The cooking should be done in a double boiler. The artichoke also makes a very good soup.

FRENCH ARTICHOKES WITH TOMATO SAUCE

Pick off from the solid green globes the outer tough petals. Scoop out with a sharp-pointed knife the fuzzy centres, leaving the soft base, which is the luscious morsel. Cut each artichoke in halves, wash, drain and fry brown on each side in olive oil Make tomato sauce and cook thirty minutes in that mixture. Then serve.

BEET GREENS

Beets are usually thickly sowed, and as the young plants begin to grow they must be thinned out. These plants make delicious greens, and even the tops of the ordinary market beets are good if properly prepared. Examine the leaves carefully to be sure that there are no insects on them; wash thoroughly in several waters, and put over the fire in a large kettle of boiling water. Add one teaspoon of salt for every two quarts of greens; boil rapidly about thirty minutes or until tender; drain off the water; chop well and season with butter and salt.

BOILED BEETS

Carefully wash any earth off the beets, but every care is needed to avoid breaking the skin, roots or crown; if this is done much of their color will be lost, and they will be a dull pink. Lay them in plenty of boiling water, with a little vinegar; boil them steadily, keeping them well covered with water for about one and one-half to two hours for small beets and two to three and one-half hours for large ones. If they are to be served hot, cut off the roots and crown and rub off the skin directly, but if to be served cold, leave them until they have become cold and then cut into thin slices and sprinkle with salt and pepper and pour some vinegar over them. If to be eaten hot, cut them into thin slices, arrange them on a hot vegetable dish and pour over white sauce or melted butter, or hand these separately.

BAKED BEETS

Boil large beetroot about two hours, being careful not to pierce it. When cold mash very smooth, add a little drippings, pepper, salt and stock. Place in a greased pan and bake one hour.

SOUR BUTTERED BEETS

Wash as many beets as required and cook in bailing water until tender. Drain and turn into cold water for peeling. Remove the skins, slice and sprinkle with as much salt as desired. Melt one-half cup of butter in a large frying-pan and add two tablespoons of strained lemon juice. Stir the butter and lemon juice until blended, keeping the fire low. Now turn the beets into this sauce, cover the pan and shake and toss until the sauce has been well distributed. Serve hot at once.

CELERIAC

This vegetable is also known as "knot celery" and "turnip-rooted celery." The roots, which are about the size of a white turnip, and not the stalks are eaten. They are more often used as a vegetable than as a salad.

Pare the celeriac, cut in thin, narrow slices, and put into cold water. Drain from this water and drop into boiling water and boil thirty minutes. Drain and rinse with cold water. The celeriac is now ready to be prepared and served the same as celery.

PURÉE OF CELERIAC

Boil as directed above and press through a sieve. To one quart take two tablespoons of butter blended with two tablespoons flour and cooked until smooth and frothy, add the strained celeriac and cook five minutes, stirring frequently. Add one teaspoon of salt and a half cup of cream, cook five minutes longer and serve hot on toast or fried bread.

CAULIFLOWER

Trim off the outside leaves and cut the stalk even with the flower. Let it stand upside down in cold salted water for twenty minutes. Put it into a generous quantity of rapidly boiling salted water and cook it uncovered about twenty minutes or until tender, but not so soft as to fall to pieces. Remove any scum from the water before lifting out the cauliflower. If not perfectly white, rub a little white sauce over it. Serve with it a white, a Bechamel, or a Hollandaise sauce; or it may be served as a garnish to chicken, sweetbreads, etc., the little bunches being broken off and mixed with the sauce.

SPANISH CAULIFLOWER

Finely chop one medium-size onion and a small bunch of parsley. Melt one tablespoon butter in a pan and fry the onion until it is brown. Season with celery salt. Blend in one tablespoon flour, add one cup boiling water and let simmer for half an hour. Carefully clean the cauliflower and boil for one-half hour. Drain the onion sauce, add three tablespoons tomato catsup, drain the cauliflower, turn into a baking-pan, pour over the sauce, place in a moderate oven for five minutes and serve hot.

CAULIFLOWER WITH BROWN CRUMBS

Drain and place the hot cauliflower in serving dish, and pour over it two tablespoons fine bread crumbs browned in one tablespoon of hot butter or fat. Serve hot. Asparagus may be served in this style.

CAULIFLOWER OR ASPARAGUS (HUNGARIAN)

Cook in salt water until tender. Spread with bread crumbs and butter. Pour some sour cream over the vegetable and bake until the crumbs are a golden brown.

SCALLOPED CAULIFLOWER

Boil and drain off the water, grease a baking-dish, line with a layer of cauliflower, add a layer of toasted bread crumbs, another of cauliflower and so on alternately, letting the top layer be of bread crumbs. Over all pour one cup of boiling milk, dot the top with butter and bake in a moderate oven for twenty minutes.

CAULIFLOWER (ROUMANIAN)

Brown a minced onion, add cauliflower cut in pieces with a small quantity of water; stew, add salt, white pepper, a little sour salt and red tomatoes; when half done add one-fourth cup of rice. Cook until rice is done. The onion may be browned either in butter, fat or olive oil, as desired.

CREAMED CELERY

Remove the leaves from the stalks of celery; scrape off all rusted or dark spots; cut into small pieces and drop in cold water. Having boiling water ready; put the celery into it, adding one-half teaspoon of salt for every quart of water. Boil until tender, leaving the cover partly off; drain and rinse in cold water. Make a cream sauce; drop the celery into it; heat thoroughly and serve.

LETTUCE

If lettuce has grown until rather too old for salad, it may be cooked, and makes a fairly palatable dish.

BOILED LETTUCE

Wash four or five heads of lettuce, carefully removing thick, bitter stalks and retaining all sound leaves. Cook in plenty of boiling salted water for ten or fifteen minutes, then blanch in cold water for a minute or two. Drain, chop lightly, and heat in stew-pan with some butter, and salt and pepper to taste. If preferred, the chopped lettuce may be heated with a pint of white sauce seasoned with salt, pepper, and grated nutmeg. After simmering for a few minutes in the sauce, draw to a cooler part of the range and stir in the well-beaten yolks of two eggs.

GREEN LIMA BEANS

Cover the shelled beans with boiling water; bring to a boil quickly; then let them simmer slowly till tender. Drain and add salt, pepper and butter or hot cream or cream sauce.

CARROTS

Scrape the carrots lightly; cut them into large dice or slices and drop them into salted boiling water, allowing one teaspoon of salt to one quart of water. Boil until tender; drain and serve with butter and pepper or with cream sauce.

LEMON CARROTS

Old carrots may be used for this dish, and are really better than the new ones. Pare and cut into dice, and simmer in salted water until tender, but not pulpy. Drain, return to the fire, and for one pint of carrots add one teaspoon of minced parsley, a grating of loaf sugar, one-half teaspoon of paprika, one tablespoon of butter and the juice of half a lemon. Heat through, shaking the dish now and then, so that each piece of the vegetable will be well coated with the mixture or dressing.

SIMMERED CARROTS

Wash, scrape and slice one quart carrots roundwise. Put them in a saucepan with one tablespoon of butter or drippings, three tablespoons of sugar and one teaspoon salt. Cover closely and let simmer on a slow fire until tender.

FLEMISH CARROTS

Scrape, slice and cook one quart of carrots in one quart of boiling water to which has been added one teaspoon of salt, until tender; drain. Heat two tablespoons fat, add one small onion, brown lightly, add the carrots, season with one teaspoon of sugar, one-quarter teaspoon of salt, one-eighth teaspoon of white pepper and shake well over the fire for ten minutes, add one and one-half cups of soup stock, cover and simmer for one-half hour, then add one teaspoon chopped parsley and serve hot.

CARROTS WITH BRISKET OF BEEF

Salt and pepper two pounds of fat brisket of beef and let stand several hours. Wash and scrape two bunches of carrots and cut in small cubes. Place in kettle with meat, cover with boiling; water and cook several hours or until the meat and carrots are tender, and the water is half boiled away. Heat two tablespoons of fat in a spider, let brown slightly, add two tablespoons of flour and gradually one cup of carrot and meat liquid. Place in kettle with meat and carrots and boil until carrots become browned.

COMPOTE OF CARROTS (RUSSIAN STYLE)

Make a syrup of one cup of sugar and one cup of water by boiling ten minutes. To this syrup add two cups of carrots diced, which have previously been browned in two tablespoons hot fat or butter. Cook all together until carrots are tender. Brown in oven and serve.

CORN ON THE COB

Free the corn from husks and silk; have a kettle of water boiling hard; drop the corn into it and cook ten minutes (or longer if the corn is not young). If a very large number of ears are put into the water they will so reduce the temperature that a longer time will be needed. In no case, however, should the corn be left too long in the water, as overcooking spoils the delicate flavor.

CORN OFF THE COB

Corn is frequently cut from the cob after it is cooked and served in milk or butter; but by this method much of the flavor and juke of the corn itself is wasted; It is better to cut the corn from the cob before cooking. With a sharp knife cut off the grains, not cutting closely enough to remove any of the woody portion of the skins. Then with a knife press out all the pulp and milk remaining in the cob; add this to the corn; season well with salt, pepper and butter; add a little more milk if the corn is dry; cook, preferably in the oven, for about ten minutes, stirring occasionally. If the oven is not hot, cook over the fire.

SUCCOTASH

Mix equal parts of corn, cut from the ear, and any kind of beans; boil them separately; then stir them lightly together, and season with butter, salt, and pepper and add a little cream if convenient.

CANNED CORN

To one can of corn take one tablespoon of butter, one-half cup milk; sprinkle one tablespoon of flour over these; stir and cook about five minutes, until thoroughly hot. Season to taste and serve hot.

DANDELIONS

Wash one peck of dandelions; remove roots. Cook one hour in two quarts of boiling salted water. Drain, chop fine; season with salt, pepper and butter. Serve with vinegar.

STUFFED CUCUMBERS

Cut four cucumbers in half lengthwise; remove the seeds with a spoon, lay the cucumbers in vinegar overnight; then wipe dry and fill with a mixture made from one cup pecans or Brazil nuts chopped, six tablespoons of mashed potatoes, one well-beaten egg, one teaspoon of salt, two tablespoons of chopped parsley, one saltspoon of white pepper, dash of nutmeg and two tablespoons of melted butter. Bake in a buttered dish until tender. Serve hot with one cup of white sauce, dash of powdered cloves, one well-beaten egg, salt and pepper to taste.

FRIED CUCUMBERS

Daintily prepared fried cucumbers are immeasurably superior to fried egg plant and are especially nice with boiled chicken.

Peel and slice the cucumbers lengthwise in about the same thickness observed with egg plant. Lay these slices in salt and water for about an hour, then dip in beaten egg and cracker dust, and French fry in boiling fat, taking care to carefully drain in a colander before serving.

COLD SLAW

Take a firm, white head of cabbage; cut it in halves; take out the heart and cut as fine as possible on slaw-cutter. Cut up one onion at the same time and a sour apple. Now sprinkle with salt and white pepper and a liberal quantity of white sugar. Mix this lightly with two forks. Heat one tablespoon of goose oil or butter, and mix it thoroughly in with the cabbage. Heat some white wine vinegar in a spider; let it come to a boil and pour over the slaw, boiling. Keep covered for a short time. Serve cold.

BOILED SAUERKRAUT

Take brisket of beef weighing about two or three pounds. Set it on to boil in two quarts of water, a little salt and the usual soup greens. When the meat is tender take it out, salt it well and put on to boil again in a porcelain-lined kettle, having previously removed all the bones. Add about a cup of the soup stock and as much sauerkraut as you desire. Boil about one hour; tie one tablespoon of caraway seed in a bag and boil in with the kraut. Thicken with two raw potatoes, grated, and add one tablespoon of brown sugar just before serving. If not sour enough add a dash of vinegar. This gives you meat, vegetables and soup. Mashed potatoes, kartoffelkloesse or any kind of flour dumpling is a nice accompaniment. Sauerkraut is just as good warmed over as fresh, which may be done two or three times in succession without injury to its flavor.

TO BOIL CABBAGE

Cut a small head of cabbage into four parts, cutting down through the stock. Soak for half an hour in a pan of cold water to which has been added one tablespoon of salt; this is to draw out any insects that may be hidden in the leaves. Take from the water and cut into slices. Have a large stew-pan half full of boiling water; put in the cabbage, pushing it under the water with a spoon. Add one tablespoon of salt and cook from twenty-five to forty-five minutes, depending upon the age of the cabbage. Turn into a colander and drain for about two minutes. Put in a chopping bowl and mince. Season with butter, pepper, and more salt if it requires it. Allow one tablespoon of butter to a generous pint of the cooked vegetable. Cabbage cooked in this manner will be of delicate flavor and may be generally eaten without distress. Have the kitchen windows open at the top while the cabbage is boiling, and there will be little if any odor of cabbage in the house.

FRIED CABBAGE

Cut one medium head of cabbage fine, soak ten minutes in salt water. Drain, heat three tablespoons of fat (from top of soup stock preferred), add cabbage, one sour apple peeled and cut up, caraway seed to taste, salt, paprika and one-half onion minced. Cover very closely and cook slowly for one hour.

CREAMED NEW CABBAGE

To one pint of boiled and minced new cabbage add one-half pint of hot milk, one tablespoon of butter, one teaspoon of flour, one-half teaspoon each of salt and pepper, one teaspoon finely minced parsley and a generous dash of sweet paprika. The butter and flour should be creamed together before stirring in. Let simmer for about ten minutes, stirring occasionally to keep from burning. Serve hot on toasted bread.

HOT SLAW

Cut the cabbage into thin shreds as for cold slaw. (Use a plane if convenient). Boil it until tender in salted fast-boiling water. Drain it thoroughly, and pour over it a hot sauce made of one tablespoon of butter, one-half teaspoon of salt, dash of pepper and of cayenne, and one-half to one cup of vinegar, according to its strength. Cover the saucepan and let it stand on the side of the range for five minutes, so that the cabbage and sauce will become well incorporated.

CARROTS BOILED WITH CABBAGE

Pare the carrots and cut them into finger lengths, in thin strips. Put a breast of lamb or mutton on to boil, having previously salted it well. When boiling, add the carrots and cover closely. Prepare the cabbage as usual and lay in with the mutton and carrots; boil two hours at least; when all has boiled tender, skim off some of the fat and put it into a spider. Add to this one tablespoon of flour, one tablespoon of brown sugar and one-half teaspoon of cinnamon. Keep adding gravy from the mutton until well mixed, and pour all over the mutton and vegetables. Serve together on a platter.

STEWED CABBAGE

Clean and drain cabbage, cut in small pieces and boil until tender. Drain and rinse in cold water; chop fine, heat one tablespoon of drippings in spider, one-fourth of an onion cut fine and one tablespoon of flour; brown all together, add one-half pint of soup stock, add cabbage and cook ten minutes longer. Salt and pepper to taste.

FILLED CABBAGE

Take a large, solid head of cabbage; take off the large top leaves, and scoop out the centre of the cabbage so as to leave the outside leaves intact for refilling. Chop your cabbage fine as for slaw; take a quarter of a loaf of stale bread, soak it in water and squeeze very dry. Heat two tablespoons of drippings in a spider, add a large-sized onion chopped fine, do not let the onion get too brown; then add the bread, one pound of chopped beef well minced and the chopped cabbage and let it get well heated; take off stove and add two eggs, pepper, salt, nutmeg, a little parsley and a little sage, season very highly. Use a little more cabbage than bread the filling. Put this all back in the cabbage, and cover this with the large leaves, put into small bread-pan and bake for two hours, put just enough water in to keep the pan from burning; don't baste. It doesn't harm if the leaves scorch.

KAL DOLMAR

Boil cabbage whole for ten minutes. Let it cool and boil the rice. Mix chopped meat, rice, and salt and pepper. Separate the cabbage leaves; put about three tablespoons of the meat and rice in the leaves, roll up and tie together with string. Then fry in fat until brown. Boil for half an hour in a little water. Make brown gravy and pour over.

SAVOY CABBAGE WITH RICE

Boil cabbage whole for five minutes; drain, separate the leaves after it has cooled. Mix one cup of boiled rice with three dozen raisins, pinch of salt, one teaspoon of cinnamon and two tablespoons of drippings. Put two tablespoons of this mixture in three or four leaves, roll them and tie together with string. Place in pan and let cook for an hour until done. This dish is just as good warmed up a second time.

There must be sufficient fat and gravy to prevent the cabbage rolls from sticking to the bottom of the pan which must be kept closely covered.

BELGIAN RED CABBAGE

Put two or three sticks of cinnamon, salt and pepper, one-half teaspoon cloves, one onion sliced thin, one bay leaf, two cups of water, three tablespoons of drippings in saucepan, then add five or six greening apples, peeled and cut in quarters. Lastly, put in one medium-sized red cabbage, cut in halves and then sliced very thin. Cook three hours and then add two tablespoons each of sugar and vinegar; cook one minute more.

RED CABBAGE

Cut fine on slaw-cutter, put cabbage in a colander, pour boiling water over it and let it stand over another pan for ten minutes; salt, mix well, and cut up a sour apple in the cabbage. Heat one tablespoon goose or soup drippings, brown in this an onion cut fine, add the cabbage and stew slowly, keep covered. Add a little hot water after it has boiled about five minutes. When tender add a few cloves, vinegar, brown sugar and cinnamon to taste, and serve. White cabbage may be cooked in this way.

RED CABBAGE WITH CHESTNUTS AND PRUNES

Clean cabbage and cut off outside leaves, cut on cabbage-cutter—blanch as above. Take one tablespoon of butter, put in kettle and let brown, add cabbage, let simmer about ten minutes, stir and let simmer ten minutes more. Add about one cup of water, one-fourth cup of vinegar, and one tablespoon of sugar, salt and pepper to taste. Add one-fourth cup of raisins and blanched chestnuts and cook until tender, adding to cabbage just before serving. Take one tablespoon of flour smooth with cold water, add to cabbage, let cook a few minutes and serve.

VEGETABLE HASH

Hash may be made with one or many vegetables and with or without the addition of meat and fish. Potato is the most useful vegetable for hash, because it combines well with meat or other vegetables. The vegetables must be chopped fine, well seasoned with salt and pepper, and parsley, onion, chives or green pepper if desired, and moistened with stock, milk or water, using a quarter of a cup to a pint of hash. Melt one-half tablespoon of butter or savory drippings in a pan; put in the hash, spreading it evenly and dropping small pieces of butter or drippings over the top. Cover the pan; let the hash cook over a moderate fire for half an hour; fold over like an omelet and serve. If properly cooked there will be a rich brown crust formed on the outside of the hash.

BAKED EGGPLANT

Parboil eggplant until tender, but not soft, in boiling salted water. Cut in half crosswise with a sharp knife. Scrape out the inside and do not break the skin.

Heat one tablespoon of butter, add a minced onion, brown, then scraped eggplant, bread crumbs, salt and pepper to taste and an egg yolk. Mix well together, refill shells, place in dripping pan in oven—baste with butter or sprinkle cracker crumbs on top with bits of butter—baste often and brown nicely.

BROILED OR FRIED EGGPLANT

For preparing eggplant, either to fry or boil, use small eggplant as they are of more delicate flavor than the large ones. Do not cook too rapidly.

BROILED EGGPLANT

Slice the eggplant and drain it as for frying; spread the slices on a dish; season with salt and pepper; baste with olive oil; sprinkle with dried bread crumbs and broil.

EGGPLANT FRIED IN OIL (TURKISH STYLE)

Arrange in oiled pan in layers: one layer of sliced eggplant, one layer of chopped meat seasoned with egg, chopped parsley, salt and pepper; as many layers as desired, add a little olive oil, cover with water. Bake one-half hour.

EGGPLANT (ROUMANIAN)

Brown onion, peel eggplant raw, cut in quarters, put in when onions are brown with a little water and stew; add salt, white pepper, sour salt, red tomatoes; when half done add one-fourth cup of rice, cook until rice is tender.

FRIED EGGPLANT

Pare eggplant, cut in very thin slices. Sprinkle with salt, pile slices on a plate. Cover with a weight to draw out juice; let stand one hour. Dredge with flour and fry slowly in a little butter until crisp and brown, or dip in egg and cracker and fry in deep fat.

GREEN PEAS

Shell the peas and cover them with water; bring to a boil; then push aside until the water will just bubble gently. Keep the lid partly off. When the peas are tender add salt and butter; cook ten minutes longer and serve. If the peas are not the sweet variety, add one teaspoon of sugar.

SUGAR PEAS

Sugar peas may be cooked in the pods like string beans. Gather the pods while the seeds are still very small; string like beans and cut into pieces. Cover with boiling water and boil gently for twenty-five or thirty minutes

Cut boiled onions into quarters; put them in a baking dish and mix well with cream sauce; cover with bread crumbs and bits of butter and place in the oven until the crumbs are browned.

STEWED SQUASH

Peel squash, cut in quarters, put on to boil in cold water, and cook until tender. Drain, mash fine and smooth, add one-half cup of milk or cream, one tablespoon of butter, pinch of salt and pepper and put back on stove to keep hot. Beat well with a spoon to make light and smooth.

PARSNIPS

First scrape parsnips, then boil in weak salt water until tender; drain, and put in white sauce. Oyster plant may be prepared same way.

SPINACH

Spinach with large leaves is best. It is richest in mineral matter and is less liable to conceal insects that are difficult to dislodge. Buy the crisp, green spinach that has no withered leaves or stalks. That is the freshest and healthiest.

Cut off the roots and pick it over carefully, cutting off all the withered leaves and stems, put the leaves in cold salt water to soak for half an hour. That refreshens them, and makes any minute insects crawl out and come to the surface. Shake the leaves about and turn them over several times, drop them in a large pan of water; rinse well; lift them out separately and drop back into a second pan of water. Continue washing in fresh water until there is not a grain of sand to be found in the bottom of the pan.

In cooking be careful not to put too much water in the pot. That is the trouble with most spinach. It is drowned in water; a cup is plenty for one quart of spinach. Let the water come to a boil. Then lift the spinach out of the pan with the cold water dripping from it and put it into the pot, into the boiling water. Put the lid on the pot. Turn the fire a little low and let it cook slowly for fifteen minutes, stirring every now and then to keep it from sticking to the bottom of the pot.

Just before taking up the spinach put some salt in it; then drain off the water and put a big tablespoon of butter and one-quarter teaspoon of pepper in it. Take it out of the pot and place it in a long, flat dish. Slice some hard-boiled eggs and place the slices all around the spinach for a kind of border.

SPINACH WITH CREAM SAUCE

Cook as directed, drain through colander, and grind through machine, make a rich cream sauce. Stir spinach in this sauce, add pepper, salt, nutmeg to taste, and garnish with slices of hard-boiled egg.

SPINACH—FLEISCHIG

Boil a quart of spinach about fifteen minutes, drain thoroughly through a colander and chop extremely fine. Heat one tablespoon of drippings in a saucepan, rub one tablespoon of flour in it, add salt, pepper and ginger to taste. Add one cup of soup stock to the whole or some beef gravy. Put the spinach in the sauce, let boil for five minutes. Garnish with hard-boiled eggs or use only the hard-boiled whites for decoration, rub the yolks to a powder and mix through the spinach.

SAVOY CABBAGE

Cut off the faded outside leaves and hard part of the stalk, and wash the vegetable well. Cook in boiling salted water. Drain, chop very fine and proceed as with spinach in the foregoing recipe.

BRUSSELS SPROUTS

Remove any wilted leaves from the outside of the sprouts, and let them stand in cold salted water from fifteen to twenty minutes. Put the sprouts into salted, rapidly boiling water and cook, uncovered, fifteen or twenty minutes or until tender, but not until they lose their shape. Drain them thoroughly in a colander; then place them in a saucepan with butter, pepper and salt, and toss them until seasoned; or mix them lightly with just enough white sauce to coat them.

OYSTER PLANT—SALSIFY

Wash, scrape and put at once in cold water with a little vinegar to keep from discoloring. Cut one-half inch slices and cook in boiling, salted water until soft. Drain and serve in white sauce. Or boil in salted, boiling water until tender and cut in four pieces lengthwise, dredge with flour and sprinkle with a little salt and fry in hot butter or fat until nicely browned.

SCALLOPED SALSIFY

Boil and slice the salsify as in preceding recipe. Butter a baking dish; fill it by adding alternate layers of salsify and small bits of cheese. Season with salt, pepper and butter. Pour over it a sufficient quantity of milk or cream to moisten thoroughly. Bake one-half hour. Bread crumbs may be added if desired.

PLUMS, SWEET POTATOES AND MEAT

Wash one pound of prunes or plums and put on to boil with one pound of brisket of beef or any fat meat; when the meat is tender add five medium-sized sweet potatoes which have been pared and cut in small pieces. Place the meat on top, add one-half cup of sugar and a piece of sour salt (citric acid). Cover and bake until nicely browned. If gravy should cook away add some warm water.

TSIMESS

Take equal portions of parboiled spinach and sorrel, season to taste with ground nutmeg, pepper and salt, and add sufficient drippings to make all moist enough. Place in a covered dish in a slow oven.

This is prepared on Friday and left in the oven to keep hot until needed for Shabbas dinner. All green vegetables may be prepared in the same way.

TURNIPS

Do not spoil turnips by overcooking. The flat white summer turnip when sliced will cook in thirty minutes. The winter turnip requires from forty-five to sixty minutes.

BOILED TURNIPS

Have the turnips peeled and sliced. Drop the slices into a stew-pan with boiling water enough to cover generously. Cook until tender, then drain well. They are now ready to mash or chop. If they are to be served mashed, put them back in the stew-pan; mash with a wooden vegetable masher, as metal is apt to impart an unpleasant taste. Season with salt, butter, and a little pepper. Serve at once.

HASHED TURNIPS

Chop the drained turnips into rather large pieces. Return to the stew-pan, and for one and one-half pints of turnips add one teaspoon of salt, one-fourth teaspoon of pepper, one tablespoon of butter, and four tablespoons of water. Cook over a very hot fire until the turnips have absorbed all the seasonings. Serve at once. Or the salt, pepper, butter, and one tablespoon of flour may be added to the hashed turnips; then the stew-pan may be placed over the hot fire and shaken frequently to toss up the turnips. When the turnips have been cooking five minutes in this manner add one-half pint of meat stock or of milk and cook ten minutes.

When meat or soup stock is used substitute drippings for the butter in the above recipe.

KOHL-RABI WITH BREAST OF LAMB

Strip off the young leaves and boil in salt water. Then peel the heads thickly, cut into round, thin slices, and lay in cold water for an hour. Put on to boil a breast of mutton or lamb, which has been previously well salted, and spice with a little ground ginger. When the mutton has boiled one-half hour add the sliced kohl-rabi, and boil covered. In the meantime, drain all the water from the leaves, which you have boiled separately, and chop them, but not too fine, and add them to the mutton. When done thicken with flour, season with pepper and more salt if needed. You may omit the leaves if you are not fond of them.

KOHL-RABI

Kohl-rabi is fine flavored and delicate, if cooked when very young and tender. It should be used when it has a diameter of not more than two or three inches.

Wash, peel and cut the Kohl-rabi root in dice and cook in salt water until tender. Cook the greens or tops in another pan of boiling water until tender, drain and chop very fine in a wooden bowl. Heat butter or fat, add flour, then the chopped greens, and one cup of liquor the Kohl-rabi root was cooked in or one cup of soup stock. Add the Kohl-rabi, cook altogether, and serve.

Use same quantities as for turnips.

KALE

Remove all the old or tough leaves; wash the kale thoroughly and drain. Put it into boiling water to which has been added salt in the proportion of one-half tablespoon to two quarts of water. Boil rapidly, uncovered, until the vegetable is tender; pour off the water; chop the kale very fine; return it to the kettle with one tablespoon of drippings and two of meat stock or water to every pint of the minced vegetable. Add more salt if necessary; cook for ten minutes and serve at once. The entire time for cooking varies from thirty to fifty minutes.

The leaves are sweeter and more tender after having been touched by the frost. The same is true of Savoy cabbage.

SWISS CHARD

This vegetable is a variety of beet in which the leaf stalk and midrib have been developed instead of the root. It is cultivated like spinach, and the green, tender leaves are prepared exactly like this vegetable. The midribs of the full-grown leaves may be cooked like celery.

STEWED TOMATOES

Pour boiling water over the tomatoes; remove the skins; cut into small pieces and place in a saucepan over the fire. Boil gently for twenty or thirty minutes and season, allowing for each quart of tomatoes one generous teaspoon each of salt and sugar and one tablespoon of butter. If in addition to this seasoning a slice of onion has been cooked with the tomatoes from the beginning, the flavor will be greatly improved.

CANNED TOMATOES, STEWED

Salt, pepper; add a lump of butter the size of an egg and add one tablespoon of sugar. Thicken with one teaspoon of flour wet with one tablespoon of cold water, stir into the tomatoes and boil up once.

FRIED TOMATOES

Cut large, sound tomatoes in halves and flour the insides thickly. Season with a little salt and pepper. Allow the butter to get very hot before putting in the tomatoes. When brown on one side, turn, and when done serve with hot cream or thicken some milk and pour over the tomatoes hot.

FRIED GREEN TOMATOES

Cut into thin slices large green tomatoes, sprinkle with salt and dip into cornmeal, fry slowly in a little butter till well browned; keep the frying-pan covered while they are cooking, so they will be perfectly tender. These are very delicately flavored, and much easier to fry than ripe tomatoes. They make an excellent breakfast dish.

TOMATO PURÉE

Scald the tomatoes, take off the skins carefully and stew with one teaspoon each of butter and sugar; salt and pepper to taste. This is enough seasoning for a quart of tomatoes. When the tomatoes are very soft strain through a coarse sieve and if necessary thicken with one teaspoon of flour.

SCALLOPED TOMATOES

Drain off part of the juice from one quart of tomatoes and season with pepper, salt, and onion juice. Cover the bottom of a baking dish with rolled crackers, dot over with dabs of butter, pepper, and salt, then another layer of tomatoes, then of crumbs, and so on until a layer of crumbs covers the top.

If fresh tomatoes are used bake one hour, if canned, 1/2 hour.

If the crumbs begin to brown too quickly cover the dish with a tin plate.

STUFFED TOMATOES

Select tomatoes of uniform size, cut a slice from the stem end and scoop out a portion of the pulp. Have in readiness a dressing made from grated bread crumbs, parsley, a slice of minced onion, a high seasoning of salt and paprika and sufficient melted butter to moisten. Fill this into the tomatoes and heap it up in the centers. Place a bit of butter on top of each and bake in a quick oven until the vegetables are tender and the tops are delicately browned.

TOMATOES WITH RICE

Take six large tomatoes, pour boiling water over them and skin them. Scrape all the inside out with a spoon, put in saucepan together with two onions, a tablespoon of butter, one pint of water; let this boil for a little while; strain, place back on stove, pour into this one-half pound of rice, let it cook tender; add salt, pepper, a tablespoon of butter and a little grated cheese. Fill the tomatoes with this mixture, dip them in egg and bread crumbs, then fry till nice and brown.

TOMATO CUSTARDS

Simmer for fifteen minutes in a covered saucepan four cups chopped tomatoes, four eggs, one sliced onion, one bay leaf, and sprig of parsley. Strain and if there be not two cups of liquid, add water. Beat four eggs and add to liquid. Pour into greased baking cups, and stand them in a pan of water and bake until firm—about fifteen minutes. Turn out and serve with cream sauce containing green peas.

BAKED TOMATO AND EGG PLANT

Take a deep earthenware dish, pour into it a cup of cream; cut several slices of eggplant very thin, salt well, and line the dish with them; slice two large tomatoes, place a layer of these on the eggplant, next a layer of spaghetti (cooked); sprinkle with grated cheese, pieces of butter, salt, and pepper; cover this with layer of tomatoes; salt well and sprinkle with chopped green pepper, and a top layer of eggplant, which also salt and pepper well. Cook gently an hour and a half in slow, hot oven.

CREOLE TOMATOES

Take one small onion and half a green pepper, chop them fine and cook until tender in a tablespoon of butter. Cut six tomatoes in half, sprinkle with a little sugar, season on both sides with salt, pepper and a little flour, and put them into the pan with skin-side down to cook partially, then turn them once; they must cook over a slow fire. Then sprinkle one tablespoon of chopped parsley over them, pour in one cup of thick cream and when this has become thoroughly hot, and has been combined with the other ingredients, the tomatoes are ready to serve.

They have not been disturbed since the first turning and have retained their shape. Half a tomato is placed on a slice of toast, with sufficient gravy to moisten. At the season of the year, when tomatoes are hard and firm, they may be peeled before cooking. Later they will likely fall to pieces unless the skin is left on. This is one method of cooking tomatoes in which they lose the sharp acid taste, disagreeable to so many persons.

STRING BEANS WITH TOMATOES

Cut off both ends of the beans, string them carefully and break into pieces about an inch in length and boil in salt water. When tender drain off this brine and add fresh water (boiling from the kettle). Add a piece of butter, three or four large potatoes cut into squares, also four large tomatoes, cut up, and season with salt and pepper. Melt one tablespoon of butter in a spider, stir into it one tablespoon of flour, thin with milk, and add this to the beans.

STRING BEANS WITH LAMB

Take a small breast of lamb, two large onions, one-quarter peck of beans (string and cut in long thin pieces); skin six large tomatoes, and add two cups of water. Cook until the beans are tender, then add one tablespoon of flour to thicken.

STRING OR WAX-BEANS, SWEET AND SOUR

Put the beans into sufficient boiling water to just cover them; cook for one hour and a half to two hours, depending upon the tenderness of the beans. Meanwhile, prepare for each quart of beans five sour apples; peel, core and cut in pieces. When the beans are done, add the apples, the thin peel of one lemon, the juice of one and one-half lemons, a small teaspoon of salt, and two tablespoons of cider vinegar. Let the apples cook on top of the beans until they are thoroughly done, then mix well with a good quarter cup of granulated sugar. This dish will be better by being served the next day warmed up.

SWEET SOUR BEANS

If you use canned string beans, heat some fat in a spider and put in one tablespoon of flour; brown slightly; add one tablespoon of brown sugar, a pinch of salt, some cinnamon and vinegar to taste; then add the beans and let them simmer on the back of stove, but do not let them burn. The juice of pickled peaches or pears is delicious in preparing sweet and sour beans.

STRING OR GREEN SNAP BEANS

Cut off the tops and bottoms and "string" carefully; break the beans in pieces about an inch long and lay them in cold water, with a little salt, for ten or fifteen minutes. Heat one tablespoon of drippings in a stew-pan, in which you have cut up part of an onion and some parsley; cover this and stew about ten minutes. In the meantime, drain the beans, put into the stew-pan and stew until tender; add one tablespoon of flour and season with salt and pepper (meat gravy or soup stock will improve them). You may pare about half a dozen potatoes, cut into dice shape, and add to the beans. If you prefer, you may add cream or milk instead of soup stock and use butter.

POTATOES

Potatoes are valuable articles of food and care should be taken in cooking them. The most economical method is to cook them in their "jackets" as there is not nearly as much waste of potato or of the salts that are valuable as food.

POTATOES BOILED IN THEIR JACKETS

Potatoes should be well brushed and put on to boil in a saucepan of boiling water; they should continue boiling at the same degree of heat until they are done, when a fork will easily pierce them. This will take from twenty-five to thirty minutes. Drain, draw the saucepan to a low flame, place a clean cloth folded over the top of the saucepan and press the lid down over it.

This dries the potatoes and makes them a good color. Hold the potatoes in a cloth and peel them, then reheat for one minute and serve.

New potatoes, if well brushed or scraped do not require peeling.

POTATOES FOR TWENTY PEOPLE

To serve twenty people one-half peck of potatoes is required.

BOILED POTATOES

Peel six or eight potatoes, and put them on in boiling water to which has been added one teaspoon of salt. Boil as above.

The saucepan used for cooking potatoes should be used for no other purpose.

BAKED POTATOES, No. 1

Select fine, smooth potatoes and boil them about twenty minutes. Drain off the water, remove the skins and pack in a buttered dish. Lay a small piece of butter on each potato, sprinkle with salt and pepper, and sprinkle fine bread crumbs over all, with a few tablespoons of cream. Bake until a nice light brown. Serve in the same dish. Garnish with parsley.

BAKED POTATOES, No. 2

Wash large potatoes and bake in a quick oven until soft, which will take about three-quarters of an hour. This is the most wholesome way of cooking potatoes.

POTATO BALLS WITH PARSLEY

Pare very thin, medium potatoes as near a size as possible. Have ready a pot of boiling water, salted, drop in the potatoes and keep them at a quick boil until tender. Serve with a batter made by beating to a cream two tablespoons of butter, one-half tablespoon of lemon juice and one tablespoon of finely minced parsley; add salt and a dash of cayenne pepper; spread over the hot potatoes, and it will melt into a delicious dressing. This is especially nice to serve with fish.

NEW POTATOES

Brush and scrape off all the skin of six potatoes and boil for half an hour in salted boiling water, drain, salt and dry for a few minutes, and then pour melted butter over them and sprinkle with chopped parsley.

MASHED POTATOES

Old potatoes may be used. Pare as many potatoes as required. Boil in salt water, drain thoroughly when done and mash them in the pot with a potato masher, working in a large tablespoon of butter and enough milk to make them resemble dough, do not allow any lumps to form in your dish. Garnish with parsley.

SCALLOPED POTATOES, No. 1

Grease a pan with butter. Choose the potatoes that are so big or misshapen you wouldn't want to use them for boiling or baking. Cut them in thin slices. Spread them in the pan in a layer an inch thick. Sprinkle with pepper and salt to taste. Dot with butter here and there, perhaps a half teaspoon for each layer. Four or six bits of butter should be sprinkled over each layer. Repeat the layers of the raw potatoes until the pan is full. Cover them with milk. Place in the oven and cook for one hour.

SCALLOPED POTATOES, No. 2

Cut two cups of cold potatoes into cubes; mix well with two cups of cream sauce, adding more seasoning if necessary; pour into a baking dish; cover with one cup of bread crumbs and dot with small pieces of butter and bake for about half an hour.

ROAST POTATOES

Take either sweet or Irish potatoes, or both; pare, wash, and salt them, and lay them around the meat, and let them roast for about three-quarters of an hour. Turn them about once, so they will be nicely browned.

CREAMED POTATOES

Make a cream sauce, a little thinner than usual by adding a little extra milk. Cut two cups of boiled potatoes into small cubes and mix them thoroughly with the same. Cook in a double boiler until the potatoes are thoroughly hot, add a little chopped parsley if desired, and serve.

POTATOES AU GRATIN

Slice two cups of cold boiled potatoes and add them to two cups of hot cream sauce. Bring all to a boil; remove and add three tablespoons of grated cheese, salt and pepper to taste. Pour all into a baking dish, sprinkle buttered bread crumbs over the top and set in the oven to brown.

GERMAN FRIED POTATOES

Cut up some raw potatoes quite thin, salt and pepper and drop in boiling fat. Cover up at first to soften them. Turn frequently to prevent burning and then remove the cover to brown slightly.

SARATOGA CHIPS

Proceed as above; but do not cover and do not take as many potatoes at one time.

HASHED BROWN POTATOES, LYONNAISE

Finely hash up six cold boiled potatoes and keep on a plate. Heat one tablespoon of butter in a frying-pan, add a finely chopped onion, and lightly brown for three minutes, then add the potatoes. Season with one-half teaspoon of salt and two saltspoons of white pepper, evenly sprinkled over, then nicely brown them for ten minutes, occasionally tossing them meanwhile. Give them a nice omelet form, brown for eight minutes more, turn on a hot dish, sprinkle a little freshly chopped parsley over and serve. These potatoes may be prepared with fat in place of butter.

CURRIED POTATOES

Melt two tablespoons of fat in a frying-pan; add one onion chopped fine and cook until straw color. Add two cups of boiled potatoes, cut in dice, one-half cup of stock, and one tablespoon of curry powder. Cook until the stock has been absorbed; then add one-half teaspoon of salt, a dash of red pepper, and one teaspoon of lemon juice.

POTATO CAKES

Take cold mashed potatoes or cold baked or boiled potatoes that have been mashed and seasoned; roll into balls, dusting the hands well with flour first. Flatten into cakes and sauté in butter, or place on a buttered tin with a small piece of butter on the top of each and bake in a hot oven until golden brown.

POTATOES AND CORN

Butter well a deep baking dish, holding a quart or more. In the bottom place a layer of potatoes, sliced thin, then a layer of corn, using one-half the contents of a can. On this sprinkle a little grated onion and season with salt, pepper and bits of butter. Add another layer of potatoes, then the rest of the corn, seasoning as before, and cover the whole with a layer of cracker crumbs. Dot well with butter, pour on milk until it comes to the top, and bake three-quarters of an hour. Use cooked potatoes, having them cold before slicing.

FRENCH FRIED POTATOES

Pare the potatoes and throw them into cold water until needed. Dry them with a towel; cut into small pieces lengthwise of the potato; drop them into hot fat and remove when lightly browned. It is better to fry only a few at a time, letting those done stand in a colander in the oven to keep hot. When all are done, sprinkle with salt and serve at once.

For variety; and for use in garnishing, cut the potatoes into balls, using the vegetable cutter which comes for this purpose.

POTATOES WITH CARAWAY SEEDS

Boil medium-sized potatoes in their jackets until tender, peel while hot. Put two tablespoons of butter or fat in spider, when hot add potatoes, brown well all over. Drain, sprinkle with salt and one teaspoon of caraway seeds and serve hot.

POTATOES AND PEARS

Heat two tablespoons of fat, add chopped onion and two tablespoons of flour; when flour is brown, add 1-1/2 cups of water, stir and cook until smooth, add salt, brown sugar and a little cinnamon to taste. Quarter four medium-sized cooking pears, but do not peel, cook them in the brown sauce, then add six medium, raw potatoes, pared, and cook until tender.

IMITATION NEW POTATOES

Buy a potato cutter at a first-class hardware store, and with it cut the potatoes to the size of a hickory nut, and then fry or steam them. When cooked they look just like new potatoes. They are especially nice to garnish meats. You may also parboil and brown in fat, or boil and add parsley as you would with new potatoes. The remainder of the raw potatoes may be boiled and mashed or fried into ribbons.

POTATO RIBBON

Pare and lay in cold water (ice-water is best) for half an hour. Select the largest potatoes, then cut round and round in one continuous curl-like strip (there is also an instrument for this purpose, which costs but a trifle); handle with care and fry a few at a time for fear of entanglement, in deep fat.

STEWED POTATOES WITH ONIONS

Take small potatoes, pare and wash them very clean, use one onion to about ten potatoes, add goose-oil (in fact any kind of drippings from roast meat will answer) and put them in a pot or spider. When hot cut up an onion very fine and add to the boiling fat. Then add the potatoes. Salt and pepper to taste. Pour some water over all, cover up tight and let them simmer for about 3/4 of an hour.

STEWED POTATOES, SOUR

Put a tablespoon of drippings in a kettle, and when it is hot cut up an onion fine and fry in the hot fat, cover closely. Put in potatoes, which have been previously pared, washed, quartered and well salted. Cover them tight and stew slowly until soft, stirring them occasionally. Then heat in a spider a little drippings. Brown in this a spoon of flour and add some soup-stock, vinegar and chopped parsley. Pour this over the potatoes, boil up once and serve.

STEWED POTATOES

Pare and quarter, and put on to boil. When almost done drain off the water, add one cup of milk, one tablespoon of butter, a little chopped parsley and cook a while longer. Thicken with a little flour (wet with cold water or milk), stir, and take from the fire.

STUFFED POTATOES

Take as many potatoes as are needed; when done, cut off one end and take out inside; mash this and mix with it one tablespoon of butter, a sprig of parsley, pepper, salt, and enough milk to make quite soft. Put back in tine potato skins and brown in oven and serve very hot.

If so desired the open end of each may be dipped in beaten egg before being put in oven.

BOHEMIAN POTATO PUFF

Pare, wash and boil potatoes until soft enough to mash well. Drain off nearly all the water, leaving just a little; add one teaspoon of salt and return to the stove. It is better to boil the potatoes in salt water and add more salt if necessary after mashing. Sift one-half cup of flour into the potatoes after returning to the fire and keep covered closely for about five minutes. Then remove from the stove and mash them as hard as you can, so as not to have any lumps. They must be of the consistency of dough and smooth as velvet. Now put about two tablespoons of drippings or goose-fat in a spider, chop up some onions very fine and heat them until they become a light-brown, take a tablespoon and dip it in the hot fat and then cut a spoonful of the potato dough with the same spoon and put it in the spider, and so on until you have used all. Be careful to dip your spoon in the hot fat every time you cut a puff. Let them brown slightly.

POTATOES (HUNGARIAN STYLE)

Wash, pare and cut potatoes in one-third inch pieces, there should be three cups; parboil three minutes, and drain. Add one-third cup of butter, and cook on back of range until potatoes are soft and slightly browned. Melt two tablespoons of butter, add a few drops of onion juice, two tablespoons of flour, and pour on gradually one cup of hot milk, season with salt and paprika, then add one well-beaten egg yolk. Pour sauce over potatoes and sprinkle with finely chopped parsley.

POTATO PUFF

Take two cups of cold mashed potatoes and stir into them one tablespoon of melted butter, beating to a white cream before adding anything else. Then put with this two eggs beaten extremely light, one cup of cream, and salt to taste. Beat all well and pour into a deep dish, and bake in a quick oven until it is nice and brown. If properly mixed, it will come out of the oven light, puffy, and delectable.

POTATO SURPRISE

Take large potatoes, parboil without peeling, cut a small piece of one end of the potato and scoop out the inside. Mince two ounces cooked mutton, season with pepper and salt, mix with the potato pulp and a little gravy. Return end of potato to its place and bake for about twenty minutes with a little fat on top of each potato.

BOILED SWEET POTATOES

Put on in boiling water, without any salt, and boil until a fork will easily pierce the largest. Drain off the water and dry.

FRIED SWEET POTATOES

Boil, peel and cut lengthwise into slices a quarter of an inch thick. Fry in sweet drippings or butter (cold boiled potatoes may also be fried in this way).

FRENCH FRIED SWEET POTATOES

Wash and cut small uncooked sweet potatoes into quarters; dry them and lower them into boiling hot fat. Brown thoroughly; remove with a skimmer; drain and dry on paper; sprinkle with salt and serve.

ROAST SWEET POTATOES

These are commonly called "baked" sweet potatoes. Select those of uniform size; wash, and roast in the oven until done, which you can easily tell by pressing the potatoes. If done they will leave an impression when touched. It usually requires three-quarters of an hour. Serve in their "jackets."

ROAST SWEET POTATOES WITH MEAT

Pare, cut lengthwise, salt and put them around roast meats or poultry of any kind. Roast about three-quarters of an hour, or until brown.

SWEET POTATOES AND APPLES

Wash and pare long sweet potatoes. Cook in boiling salted water until almost soft; drain and cut slices crosswise, two inches high. Core, pare and cut apples in one-half inch rounds. Into a spider, place the potatoes upright, with a slice of apple on top of each. Pour over one-half cup of maple syrup, one-fourth cup of water and two tablespoons of butter. Baste frequently until apples are soft. Then pour one teaspoon of rum over each section, place a candied cherry in the center of each apple and bake ten minutes. Remove to platter and if desired, pour more rum over and around. Light the liquor and bring to the table burning.

CANDIED SWEET POTATOES

Boil sweet potatoes, peel and cut into long slices; place in an earthen dish; place lumps of butter or chicken-fat if desired on each side, and sprinkle with sugar. A little water or juice of half a lemon may be added. Bake until the sugar and fat have candied and the potatoes are brown.

DRIED BEANS

Look the beans over carefully to remove all dirt and pebbles, then wash clean. Soak them overnight in plenty of cold water. In the morning pour off the water and put them in a stew-pan with cold water enough to cover them generously. Let them come to the boiling point in this water, then drain. If the beans are old and hard, for each quart put a piece of soda about the size of a large bean in the water in which they are soaked overnight, also in the first water in which they are boiled.

The scalded and drained beans should be put back in the stew-pan and covered generously with boiling water. Add one tablespoon of salt for one quart of beans. They should now cook slowly, with the cover partially off the stew-pan until they have reached the required degree of tenderness. For stewed and baked beans the cooking must stop when the skins begin to crack. For beans served with a sauce they should cook until perfectly tender, but they must not be broken or mushy. For purées and soups they should be cooked until very soft.

SWEET SOUR BEANS AND LINZEN

Soak overnight and drain the beans, boil in salted water until tender; drain and prepare by adding salt and pepper to taste, thicken with one tablespoon of drippings in which has been browned one tablespoon of flour and some soup stock. If the beans are to be made sweet sour add two tablespoons of vinegar and two tablespoons of brown sugar; boil for a few minutes and serve.

BAKED BEANS WITH BRISKET OF BEEF

Wash, pick over and soak overnight in cold water, two cups of navy beans. In the morning, drain and cover with fresh water, heat slowly and let cook just below the boiling point until the skins burst. When done, drain beans and put in a pot with one and one-half pounds of brisket of beef. Mix one-half tablespoon of mustard; one teaspoon of salt, one tablespoon of molasses, two tablespoons of sugar, one-half cup of boiling water and pour over beans, and add enough more boiling water to cover them. Cover pot and bake slowly six or eight hours.

HARICOT BEANS AND BEEF

Wash two cups of haricot beans and leave them covered with two pints of water overnight. Next day brown one coarsely chopped onion in a little fat and put it with the beans and their water into a casserole or stew-jar.

Cook closely covered and rather slowly in the oven or by the side of the fire one hour, then put in a pound of beef in fairly large pieces.

An hour later add one carrot cut into dice, half as many dice of turnip, and salt and pepper to taste. Continue the slow cooking until these vegetables are tender, and a few minutes before serving thicken the stew with pea meal or flour previously baked to a fawn color. Flavor with vinegar.

www.ingramcontent.com/pod-product-compliance
Lightning Source LLC
Chambersburg PA
CBHW081625100526
44590CB00021B/3603